From the Foundation Factory

Favorite
Foundation-Pieced
Minis: Book II

by Miriam Neuringer

CHITRA PUBLICATIONS

Contents

The patterns are rated according to skill level.
Look for one of these symbols with every pattern.

Easy

Intermediate

Advanced

General Directions

Patterns

Dedication

To my husband Jim,
who makes it all possible,
and to my daughter Amy,
who makes it all worthwhile.

Introduction

Welcome to *Favorite Foundation-Pieced Minis: Book II*, a pattern book featuring 10 brand new miniature quilts. I must confess that I call myself a "foundation freak." In fact, I love foundation piecing so much that it's the only technique I currently use. That's because, as a self-taught quilter, I was often disappointed with traditional piecing techniques. I never quite achieved the piecing perfection I desired and I began to find quiltmaking frustrating. All of that changed, however, when I discovered foundation piecing. Using the technique was simple and my blocks were perfect. It also put the fun back into quiltmaking. Who could ask for more?

I even began my own computer software program based on foundation piecing. I was pleased to discover that I could use computer technology to make traditional, "homey" quilts like those in this book. I designed all of them using my Quilt Pro software program. I'm excited about sharing the quilts and patterns with you in this sequel to *Favorite Foundation-Pieced Minis* (1996).

Now it's your turn to have fun. I hope you love sewing these quilts as much as I did designing them. Enjoy!

Mirian

Making your Foundations

Foundation Material Options

You can use either fabric, lightweight, non-fusible interfacing or paper for foundations. Each one has advantages that will help you decide which is best for a particular quilt.

Muslin and Interfacing: Muslin and lightweight, non-fusible interfacing are excellent foundation materials for both machine and hand stitched projects. These foundations are not removed after stitching thus they become a permanent part of the quilt. They also serve as a quilt lining, sometimes making batting unnecessary. If you plan to use sashing or borders, I suggest that you also line them with the muslin, or lightweight, non-fusible interfacing, to get a similar weight and feel. If you use batting, remember that these foundation materials add another layer to quilt through.

Paper: Paper can be used as a foundation for machine stitched projects. Paper has body so it is easy to handle. Most foundation paper available is somewhat translucent, to make it easy to see through when piecing the block. The advantage of foundation paper is that it is torn away after piecing so there is no additional bulk, making quilting easy.

Reproducing Block Designs on Foundations

There are several ways to reproduce block designs on foundation material.

Muslin and Interfacing: You can simply use a pencil and trace the design onto the foundation material or you can use a heat transfer pencil to trace the design on paper and then iron the design onto the foundation material. With the heat transfer technique, you have the advantage of making several foundations from each tracing. When you use this method, however, the pattern will be reversed. This may be important in some block patterns.

Paper: A photocopier is useful for making multiple foundations and for reducing or enlarging designs. If you want to reproduce full-size foundations, be sure the design is reproduced at 100% to avoid distortion. Check the first copy by placing it over the original to be certain there is no distortion. Trim each foundation 1" beyond the broken line after photocopying.

Another way to make paper foundations is to perforate the stitching line using a master template and your unthreaded sewing machine. It's consistent and there's no drawing or photocopying required.

• Carefully trace the block pattern to make a master template.

• Place the master template on as many as 8 to 10 layers of typing paper or 20 to 25 sheets of tracing paper.

• With an unthreaded sewing machine set at a regular stitch length (about 12 per inch), place the paper under the presser foot and carefully stitch on one line of the block to perforate it. After the first line is perforated, the papers will not shift. Continue stitching until all lines are perforated.

• Peel off the master template and set it aside for reuse. Use the perforated foundations to machine piece your block.

Piecing Your Foundations
General Instructions

• Transfer your selected foundation block pattern onto paper, muslin or lightweight, non-fusible interfacing. You will need one foundation for each block, or part of a block, in your quilt.

• The solid line is the stitching line and the broken line is the cutting line.

• Be sure to number the sections of the foundation as shown on the pattern.

• The fabric pieces you select to cover the foundation do not have to be cut precisely. Be generous when cutting fabric pieces as excess fabric will be trimmed away after sewing. Your goal is a piece that covers the numbered area and extends into surrounding areas after seams are stitched. Generally, fabric pieces should be large enough to extend 1/2" beyond the seamline on all sides before stitching. For very small sections, or sections without angles, 1/4" may be sufficient.

• Be sure that all fabric pieces around the edge of the block extend beyond the broken line so there will be enough seam allowance to set the blocks together.

• Because the foundation material acts as a stabilizer, it is less important to consider the grainline of fabric pieces that are used to make the block.

• Always stitch fabrics to block sections in numerical order. Place fabric pieces on the unmarked side of the foundation and stitch on the marked side.

• If you will be using a sewing machine, select a short stitch length, about 12 to 15 stitches per inch.

• Trim seams to 1/8" after sewing.

• Finger pressing each fabric piece after it is stitched to the foundation is sufficient for many quilt blocks but some do need more careful pressing, especially in design areas where points meet.

• If you are using a muslin or interfacing foundation, it will become a permanent part of the quilt. If you are using paper, it will be removed. However, to avoid disturbing the stitches, do not remove it until the quilt blocks have been joined together and the last border has been added to the quilt top. Use tweezers or a seam ripper to carefully remove sections of paper. The pieces will be perforated from the stitching and can be gently pulled free.

Step-by-Step Instructions

Using a foundation for the Airplane Sampler, found on page 18, let's go through each step.

Foundation Piecing Technique

The foundation piecing technique follows this simple three-step procedure:

1) position fabric pieces on the unmarked side of the foundation

2) turn the foundation over and stitch along the solid lines

3) press fabric pieces back over the seam allowance

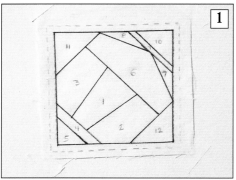

1- This is the marked foundation.

2- Center the first piece of fabric, right side up, on section 1 (airplane fuselage) on the unmarked side of the foundation. Make sure that the raw edges of the fabric extend well beyond the seamline on all sides. Holding the foundation up to a light will allow you to see the marked line through the foundation material thus helping to place the fabric piece in the correct position. A dab of glue from a glue stick, or a pin placed on the marked side of the foundation, will secure this section in place until the next section is added.

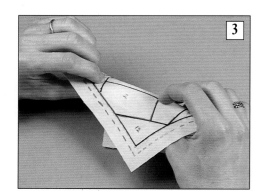

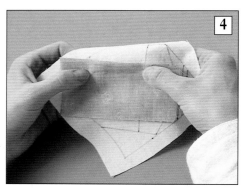

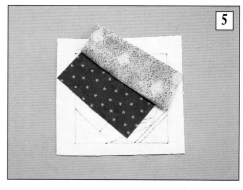

3- Select fabric for section 2 (sky). Because you will be sewing on an angle, the fabric should be at least 1/2" larger, on all sides, than the space that it will cover. Place the fabric for section 2, right sides together, with the first piece of fabric (fuselage). The seam allowance should extend approximately 1/2" beyond the stitching line.

To determine exactly where to place the second fabric: Hold the foundation in your hands with the unmarked side facing you. On the marked side of the foundation, place one finger at each corner of the stitching line.

4- Use your thumbs to hold the second fabric, right sides together, with the first fabric. You can now tip the foundation and fabric back and forth to easily see both sides of the foundation. Use your thumbs to slide the second fabric into the proper position for sewing.

5- You may want to place a pin on the seamline. Then you can fold the fabric piece over to make sure that it will cover the section and extend beyond all stitching lines. Because this piece is at the edge of the block, it should also extend beyond the broken line on the foundation. Fold the fabric piece back and remove the pin.

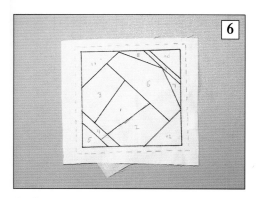

6- If needed, pin fabric into place before sewing, placing the pin on the marked side of the foundation.

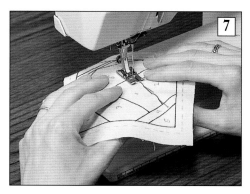

7- Carefully place the foundation and fabric on your sewing machine with the marked side of the foundation facing up.

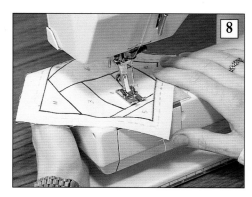

8- Sew on the line between section 1 and section 2, extending the stitching past the beginning and end of the line by a few stitches.

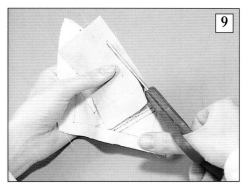

9- Fold the foundation out of the way and trim the seam allowance to 1/8".

10- Press the fabrics open.

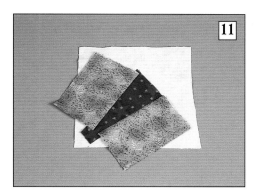

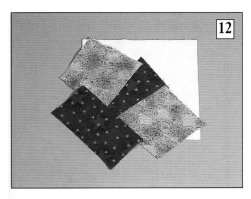

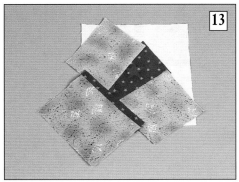

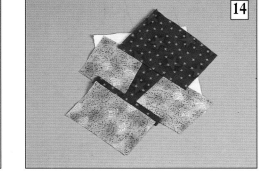

11-20- In the same way, select, align and sew fabrics to the remaining sections in numerical order. Remember that all fabrics should be cut to extend at least 1/2" beyond the seamline on all sides before stitching. Trim seams to 1/8" after sewing. Press each fabric piece as needed before moving on to the next section. Remember to stitch fabrics to the foundation in numerical order.

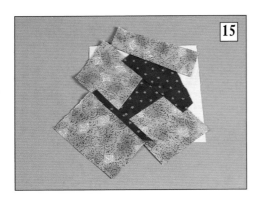

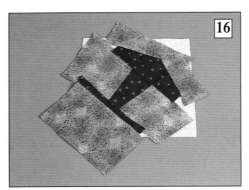

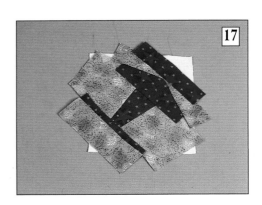

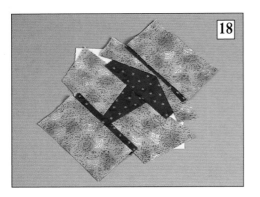

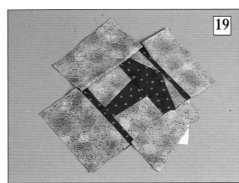

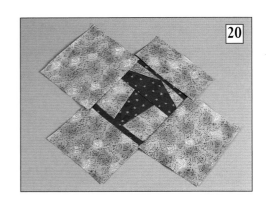

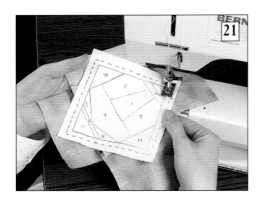

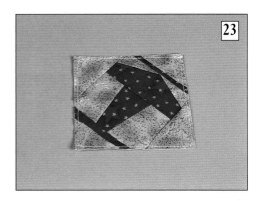

21- After all sections of the foundation are covered and the block is complete, baste the block in the seam allowance (halfway between the stitching line and the broken line) to hold all fabrics in place.

22- Trim the block on the broken line.

23- This is the completed Airplane block.

6

Stitching Tips

Fabric Selection

I recommend 100% cotton for most projects because it is easy to finger press and handles nicely. The yardage requirements in the patterns are based on a standard 44" wide bolt. However, many of the quilts can be made using fabric scraps.

Fabric Preparation

I suggest washing fabrics before using them in your minis.

Finishing The Quilt
Mitering Corners

Center each border strip on a side so the ends extend equally and sew, leaving 1/4" unstitched at the beginning and end of the stitching line. Do not stitch into the seam allowance. On the ironing board, smooth the border strips out for one corner and lay one extension over the other. Fold the top extension under at a 45° angle so the end is aligned with the strip below. Press a crease to mark the angle. Pin the ends together in several places.

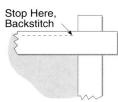

Fold the quilt on the diagonal, right sides together, and sew on the crease, starting at the seamline and running off the outer edge. Open the corner and check to see that it lies flat before trimming away excess fabric. Repeat for the remaining corners.

Batting

Use a low-loft or very thin batting. Some quilters peel batting into two layers (leaving some loft and good drape). Others use flannel as a filler. Layer the quilt sandwich as follows: backing, wrong side up; batting; quilt top, right side up. Baste or pin the layers together.

Marking and Quilting

Cut simple designs from clear plastic adhesive-backed shelf paper. They'll stick and restick long enough to finish the quilt. Use masking tape to mark grids. Remove the tape when you're not quilting to avoid leaving a sticky residue. Mark judiciously with pencils; thick lines that won't go away really stand out on a small quilt.

Very small quilts can be lap-quilted without a hoop. Larger quilts can be quilted in a hoop or small frame. Use a short, thin needle ("between") and small stitches that will be in scale with the quilt. Thread the needle with a single strand of quilting thread and knot one end. Insert the needle through the quilt top and batting (not the backing) an inch away from where you want to begin quilting. Gently pull the thread to pop the knot through the top and bury it in the batting. Too much quilting can flatten a miniature and set the quilt "out of square." Too much puffiness can detract from the scale of the quilt. Experiment and decide what you like best. When the quilting is finished, trim the backing and batting even with the top.

Binding

For most quilts, a double-fold French binding is an attractive durable and easy finish. To make 1/4" finished binding, cut each strip 1 3/4" wide on the crossgrain of the fabric. Sew binding strips together with diagonal seams; trim and press seams open.

Fold the binding strip in half lengthwise, wrong sides together, and press. Position the binding strip on the right side of the quilt top, so that all raw edges are even. Leave approximately 4" of the binding strip free. Beginning several inches from one corner, stitch the binding to the quilt with a 1/4" seam allowance. When you reach a corner, stop the stitching line exactly 1/4" from the edge of the quilt. Backstitch, clip threads and remove the quilt from the machine. Fold the binding up and away, creating a 45° angle, as shown.

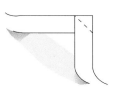

Fold the binding down as shown, and begin stitching at the quilt edge through all layers.

Continue stitching around the quilt in this manner to within 4" of the starting point. To finish, fold both strips back along the edge of the quilt so that the folded edges meet about 2" from both lines of stitching and the binding lies flat on the quilt. Finger press to crease the folds. Cut both strips 7/8" from the folds.

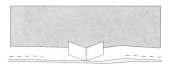

Open both strips and place the ends at right angles to each other, right sides together. Fold the quilt out of your way. Join the strips with a diagonal seam, as shown. Trim the seam to 1/4" and press it open. Fold the joined strips so that wrong sides are together again. Place the binding flat against the quilt and finish stitching it to the quilt. Trim the layers as needed so that the binding edge will be filled with batting when you fold the binding to the back of the quilt. Blindstitch the binding to the back of the quilt, covering the seamline. Remove any markings visible on the quilt top.

Sign your Quilt

Small quilts are revered by collectors, and the little quilts we make today will be treasured by our families and friends. On muslin, using embroidery, cross-stitch or permanent marker, write your name and other important data like your city, the date the quilt was completed and for whom the quilt was made. Attach it to the back of the quilt. Someone will be glad you did!

Safe at Last

This hiding place is no secret.

A perch provides a restful haven for this little red bird in **"Safe at Last"** (18" x 30"). Bright tulips decorate the garden border as the cat watches silently. This quilt is one of my favorites. (Sewn by Alice Wilhoit)

QUILT SIZE: 18" x 30"
BIRD HOUSE AND
CAT BLOCK SIZE: 6" square
TULIP BLOCK SIZE: 4" square

MATERIALS
Yardage is estimated for 44" fabric.
- 1" square black
- 2" square burgundy
- 3/8 yard green print
- 1/8 yard brown print
- 1/8 yard rose print
- 1/8 yard burgundy print
- 1/2 yard tan print
- Fat eighth (11" x 18") red print
- Fat eighth purple print
- 20" x 32" piece of backing fabric
- 20" x 32" piece of thin batting
- Paper, muslin or lightweight, non-fusible interfacing for the foundations

CUTTING
Dimensions include a 1/4" seam allowance. Fabric for foundation piecing will be cut as you sew the blocks.
- Cut 4: 4 1/2" squares, tan print
- Cut 2: 3 1/8" x 6 1/2" strips, tan print
- Cut 1: 1 1/4" x 6 1/2" strip, brown print
- Cut 2: 1 1/2" x 22 1/2" strips, burgundy print, for the inner border
- Cut 2: 1 1/2" x 10 1/2" strips, burgundy print, for the inner border
- Cut 2: 1 1/4" x 30" strips, burgundy print, for the outer border
- Cut 2: 1 1/4" x 20" strips, burgundy print, for the outer border
- Cut 3: 1 3/4" x 44" strips, green print, for the binding

DIRECTIONS
Follow the Step-by-Step Instructions *in* the General Directions *to piece the blocks.*
- Transfer the full-size patterns to the foundation material. Include all lines and numbers and leave a 1" space between foundations. Make one each of foundations 1, 2, 3, 4, 5, 6 and 7. Make 14 each of foundations 8 and 9. Cut each one out 1/2" beyond the broken line.
- Use the following fabrics in these positions:

For foundation 1:
  1 - black
  2, 3 - brown print
For foundation 2:
  1 - red print
  2 - burgundy
  3, 4 - brown print
For foundation 3:
  1 - red print
  2 - burgundy

3, 4 - brown print

For foundation 4:

   1 - tan print

   2 - red print

   3 - tan print

• Baste each foundation in the seam allowance, halfway between the stitching line and the broken line.

• Trim each foundation on the broken line.

• Stitch foundations 1, 2, 3 and 4 together to make a Bird block, as shown.

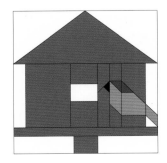

For foundation 5:

   1 - tan print

   2, 3 - brown print

   4 - Bird block

   5 - brown print

   6 - tan print

   7, 8 - brown print

   9, 10 - tan print

For foundation 6:

   1 - brown print

   2, 3 - tan print

For foundation 7:

   1 - tan print

   2, 3, 4 - purple print

   5, 6 - tan print

   7, 8 - green print

   9, 10 - tan print

   11 - green print

For foundation 8:

   1 - red print

   2, 3 - tan print

   4, 5 - rose print

   6 through 13 - tan print

For foundation 9:

   1 - green print

   2, 3 - tan print

   4, 5 - green print

   6, 7 - tan print

• Baste each foundation, as before.

• Trim each foundation on the broken line.

• Stitch foundations 5 and 6 together to make a Birdhouse block, as shown.

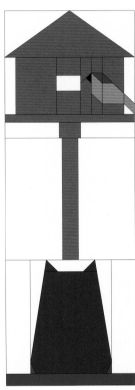

• Stitch the 1 1/4" x 6 1/2" brown print strip between 3 1/8" x 6 1/2" tan print strips to make a Post unit, as shown.

• Stitch the Post unit between the Birdhouse block and the Cat block, as shown.

• Stitch a foundation 8 and a foundation 9 together to make a Tulip block, as shown. Make 14. Set them aside.

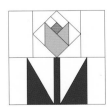

• Measure the length of the quilt. Trim the 1 1/2" x 22 1/2" burgundy print strips to equal that measurement.

• Stitch them to the sides of the quilt.

• Measure the width of the quilt, including the borders. Trim the 1 1/2" x 10 1/2" burgundy print strips to equal that measurement.

• Stitch them to the top and bottom of

the quilt.

• Stitch 5 Tulip blocks together to make a long Tulip row, as shown. Make 2.

• Stitch 2 Tulip blocks together. Make 2.

• Stitch one of these units between 4 1/2" tan print squares to make a short Tulip row, as shown. Make 2.

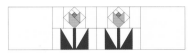

• Stitch the long Tulip rows to the sides of the quilt.

• Stitch the short Tulip rows to the top and bottom of the quilt.

• Measure the length of the quilt. Trim the 1 1/4" x 30" burgundy print strips to equal that measurement.

• Stitch them to the sides of the quilt.

• Measure the width of the quilt, including the borders. Trim the 1 1/4" x 20" burgundy print strips to equal that measurement.

• Stitch them to the top and bottom of the quilt.

• If you used paper foundations, remove them now.

• Finish according to the *General Directions*, using the 1 3/4" green print strips for the binding.

Full-Size Foundation Patterns for Safe at Last

(continued on page 10)

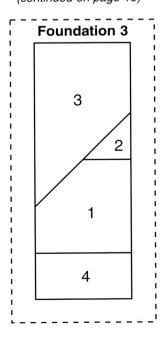

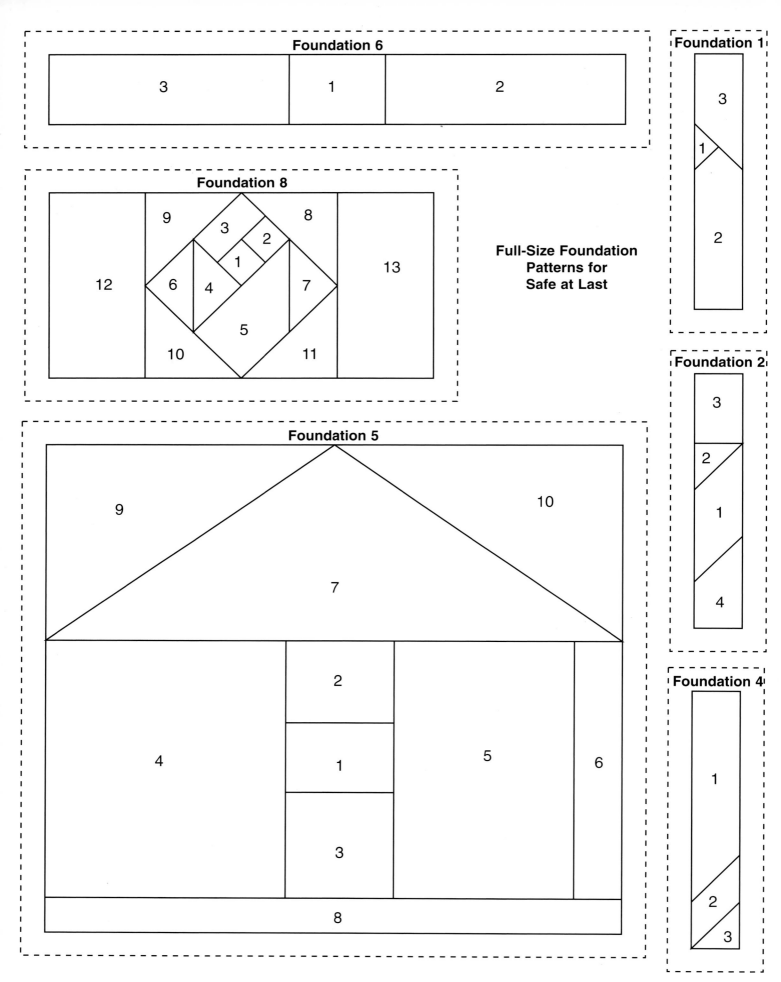

Foundation 6

3   1   2

Foundation 1

3
1
2

Foundation 8

9   3   2   8
12   1   13
6   4   7
5
10   11

Full-Size Foundation
Patterns for
Safe at Last

Foundation 2

3
2
1
4

Foundation 5

9   10
7
2
4   1   5   6
3
8

Foundation 4

1
2
3

10

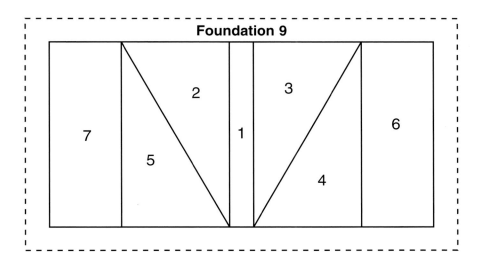

Full-Size Foundation Patterns for Safe at Last

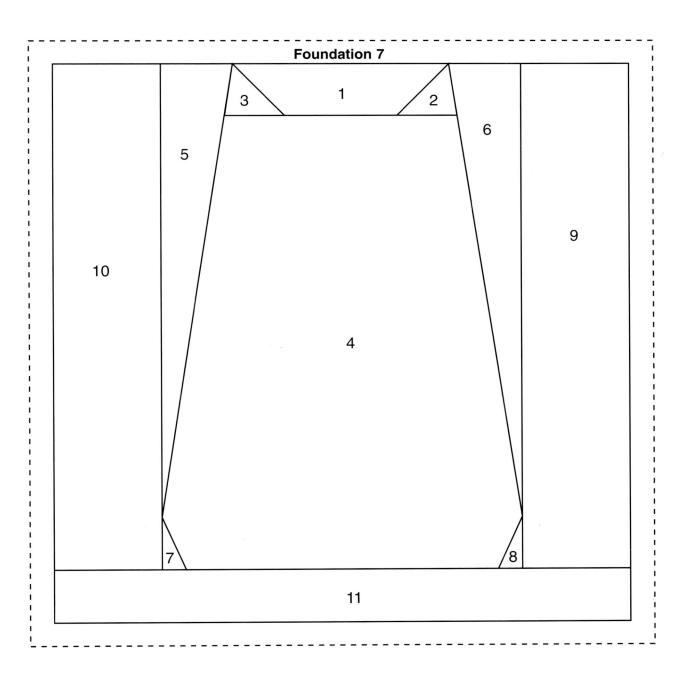

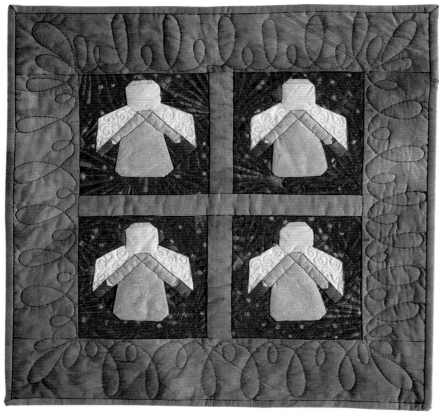

Angels at my Window

Piece a joyful heavenly choir!

Cute little cherubs float peacefully in **"Angels at my Window"** (18 3/4" square). These angels make a "perfect appearance" any time of the year. (Sewn by Christiane Meunier)

QUILT SIZE: 18 3/4" square
BLOCK SIZE: 4" square

MATERIALS
Yardage is estimated for 44" fabric.
- 5" square gold
- 8" square pink
- 4" x 6" rectangle white-on-white print
- 12" square gold print
- 5/8 yard blue print
- 1/2 yard green
- 21" square of backing fabric
- 21" square of thin batting
- Paper, muslin or lightweight, non-fusible interfacing for the foundations

CUTTING
Dimensions include a 1/4" seam allowance. Fabric for foundation piecing will be cut as you sew the blocks.
- Cut 8: 3 3/4" squares, blue print; then cut each in half diagonally to yield 16 corner triangles
- Cut 2: 1 1/2" x 6 1/8" strips, green, for the sashings
- Cut 1: 1 1/2" x 12 3/4" strip, green, for the sashing

- Cut 2: 3 1/2" x 14" strips, green, for the border
- Cut 2: 3 1/2" x 20" strips, green, for the border
- Cut 2: 1 3/4" x 44" strips, green, for the binding

DIRECTIONS
Follow the Step-by-Step Instructions *in the* General Directions *to piece the blocks.*
- Transfer the full-size patterns (found on page 17) to the foundation material. Include all lines and numbers and leave a 1" space between foundations. Make 4 each of foundations 1, 2, 3 and 4. Cut each one out 1/2" beyond the broken line.
- Use the following fabrics in these positions:

For foundations 1 and 4:
    1 - pink
    2, 3, 4 - blue print
    5 - gold print
    6 - white-on-white
    7, 8 - blue print
For foundation 2:
    1 - pink
    2 - gold

    3, 4, 5 - blue print
    6 - gold print
For foundation 3:
    1 - gold print
    2, 3, 4 - blue print
- Baste each foundation in the seam allowance, halfway between the stitching line and the broken line.
- Trim each foundation on the broken line.
- Join foundations 1, 2, 3 and 4 to make an Angel block, as shown. Make 4.

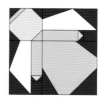

- Stitch blue print corner triangles to an Angel block, as shown. Make 4.

- Stitch 2 Angel blocks and a 1 1/2" x 6 1/8" green sashing strip together, as shown. Make 2.

 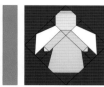

- Stitch the 1 1/2" x 12 3/4" green sashing strip between the 2 rows, referring to the photo as needed.
- Measure the length of the quilt. Trim the 3 1/2" x 14" green strips to equal that measurement.
- Stitch them to the sides of the quilt.
- Measure the width of the quilt, including the borders. Trim the 3 1/2" x 20" green strips to equal that mea-surement.
- Stitch them to the top and bottom of the quilt.
- If you used paper foundations, remove them now.
- Finish according to the *General Directions*, using the 1 3/4" green strips for the binding.
- Embellish the quilt as desired.

(Full-Size Foundation Patterns are on page 17)

(Full-Size Foundation Patterns are on page 17)

Easy

Mini Santa Quilt

Ho, Ho, Ho! St. Nick for the holidays!

"Mini Santa Quilt" (18 5/8" square) is just the right holiday dec-oration to hang on your wall or display on your mantle at Christ-mas. Draw happy faces on the Santas with a waterproof marker if you like and create a holiday mood!

QUILT SIZE: 18 5/8" square
BLOCK SIZE: 4" square

MATERIALS
Yardage is estimated for 44" fabric.
- 4" square pink
- Fat eighth (11" x 18") black
- Fat eighth white-on-white print
- Fat eighth brown print
- 1/2 yard tan print
- 3/8 yard gold print for the corner squares and binding
- 1/2 yard burgundy print
- 20 5/8" square of backing fabric
- 20 5/8" square of thin batting
- Paper, muslin or lightweight, non-fusible interfacing for the foundations

CUTTING
Dimensions include a 1/4" seam allowance. Fabric for foundation piec-ing will be cut as you sew the blocks.
- Cut 2: 1 1/2" x 8 1/2" strips, black print
- Cut 2: 1 1/2" x 10 1/2" strips, brown print
- Cut 4: 2 1/2" squares, brown print
- Cut 2: 8" squares, gold print; then cut each in half diagonally to yield 4 corner triangles
- Cut 4: 2 1/2" x 15 1/2" strips, bur-gundy print, for the border
- Cut 2: 1 3/4" x 44" strips, gold print, for the binding

DIRECTIONS
Follow the Step-by-Step Instructions *in the* General Directions *to piece the blocks.*
- Transfer the full-size patterns to the foundation material. Include all lines and numbers and leave a 1" space between foundations. Make 4 each of foundations 1, 2, 3 and 4. Cut each one out 1/2" beyond the broken line.
- Use the following fabrics in these positions:
For foundations 1 and 4:
  1 - pink
  2, 3 - tan print
  4 - burgundy print

(continued on page 14)

(continued on page 14)

13

5, 6 - tan print
For foundation 2:
    1 - white-on-white print
    2 - pink
    3 - burgundy print
    4 - white-on-white print
    5, 6 - tan print
For foundation 3:
    1 - tan print
    2, 3 - black
    4 - burgundy print
    5 - white-on-white print
    6 - burgundy print
    7, 8 - tan print

• Baste each foundation in the seam allowance, halfway between the stitching line and the broken line.
• Trim each foundation on the broken line.
• Join foundations 1, 2, 3 and 4 to make a Santa block, as shown. Make 4.

• Lay out the Santa blocks in 2 rows of 2, as shown.

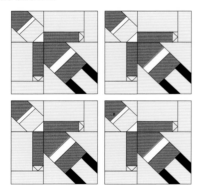

• Stitch them into rows and join the rows.

• Stitch the 1 1/2" x 8 1/2" brown print strips to opposite sides of the quilt.
• Stitch the 1 1/2" x 10 1/2" brown print strips to the remaining sides of the quilt.
• Stitch the gold print triangles to the corners of the quilt, as shown.

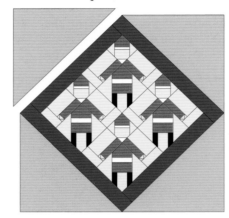

• Measure the quilt to determine the length. Trim the 2 1/2" x 15 1/2" burgundy print strips to equal that measurement.
• Stitch 2 trimmed strips to the sides of the quilt.
• Stitch a 2 1/2" brown print square to each end of a trimmed burgundy strip to make a pieced border strip, as shown. Make 2.

• Stitch the pieced border strips to the top and bottom of the quilt.
• If you used paper foundations, remove them now.
• Finish according to the *General Directions*, using the 1 3/4" gold print strips for the binding.
• Embellish the quilt as desired.

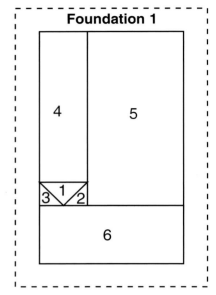

Foundation 1

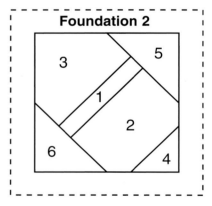

Foundation 2

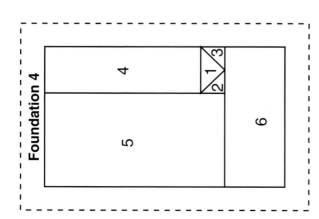

Foundation 4

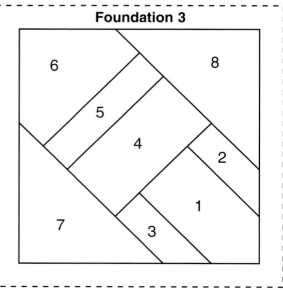

Foundation 3

Flowers and Bees

Something is buzzing besides the sewing machine!

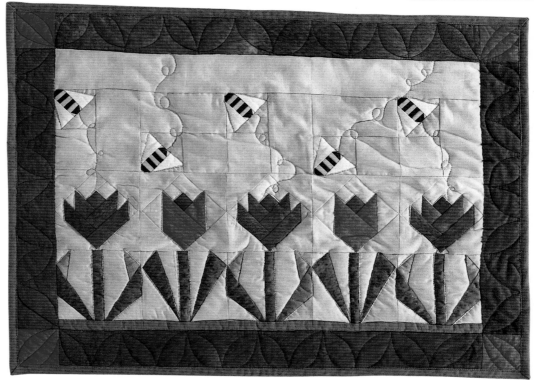

There is nothing like the smell of flowers in the garden and these bees agree! The bees add a lively rhythm to **"Flowers and Bees"** (18 1/2" x 24 1/2") which is sure to brighten your day.
(Sewn by Beth Ann Falco)

QUILT SIZE: 18 1/2" x 24 1/2"
BLOCK SIZES: 4" square

MATERIALS

Yardage is estimated for 44" fabric.
- 1 1/2 yards blue
- 2" x 10" strip white-on-white print
- 5" square gold
- 6 1/2" square black
- Fat eighth (11" x 18") red
- Fat eighth purple
- Scrap of light green at least 5" square
- Fat eighth dark green
- 1/4 yard brown print
- 20 1/2" x 26 1/2" piece of backing fabric
- 20 1/2" x 26 1/2" piece of thin batting
- Paper, muslin or lightweight, non-fusible interfacing for the foundations

CUTTING

Dimensions include a 1/4" seam allowance. Fabric for foundation piecing will be cut as you sew the blocks.
- Cut 1: 2 1/2" x 20 1/2" strip, blue
- Cut 2: 2 1/2" x 14 1/2" strips, purple
- Cut 2: 2 1/2" x 20 1/2" strips, purple
- Cut 4: 2 1/2" squares, red
- Cut 3: 1 3/4" x 44" strips, brown print

DIRECTIONS

Follow the Step-by-Step Instructions *in the* General Directions *to piece the blocks.*

- Transfer full-size patterns to the foundation material. Include all lines and numbers and leave a 1" space between foundations. Make 5 of foundation 1. Make 3 of foundation 2. Make 2 of foundation 3. Make 3 of foundation 4. Make 2 of foundation 5. Cut each one out 1/2" beyond the broken line.
- Use the following fabrics in these positions:

For foundation 1:
1 - black
2, 3 - blue
4 - gold
5 - black
6 - gold
7 - black
8 - gold
9 - black

10 - blue
11, 12 - white-on-white print
13, 14, 15, 16, 17 - blue

For foundation 2:
1 - purple
2, 3 - blue
4, 5 - purple
6, 7 - blue
8, 9 - purple
10 through 15 - blue

For foundation 3:
1 - purple
2, 3 - blue
4, 5 - red
6 through 11 - blue

For foundation 4:
1 - dark green
2, 3 - blue
4, 5 - light green
6, 7 - dark green
8, 9, 10, 11 - blue
12 - brown print

For foundation 5:
1 - dark green
2, 3 - blue
4, 5 - dark green

(continued on page 16)

15

6, 7, 8, 9 - blue
10 - brown print

- Baste each foundation in the seam allowance, halfway between the stitching line and the broken line.
- Trim each foundation on the broken line.
- Stitch the Bee blocks in a row, as shown.

- Stitch the Flower blocks in a row, as shown.

- Stitch the Stem and Leaves blocks in a row, as shown.

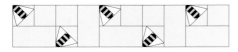

- Lay out the 2 1/2" x 20 1/2" blue strip, the Bee row, the Flower row and the Stem and Leaves row, as shown.

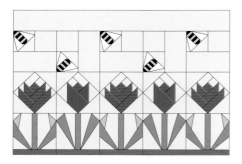

- Join the rows.
- Stitch the 2 1/2" x 14 1/2" purple strips to the sides of the quilt.
- Stitch a 2 1/2" red square to each end of a 2 1/2" x 20 1/2" purple strip to make a pieced border, as shown. Make 2.

- Stitch the pieced borders to the top and bottom of the quilt.
- If you used paper foundations, remove them now.
- Finish according to the *General Directions*, using the 1 3/4" brown print strips for the binding.

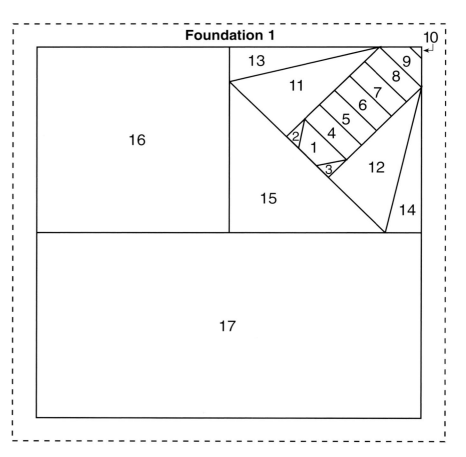

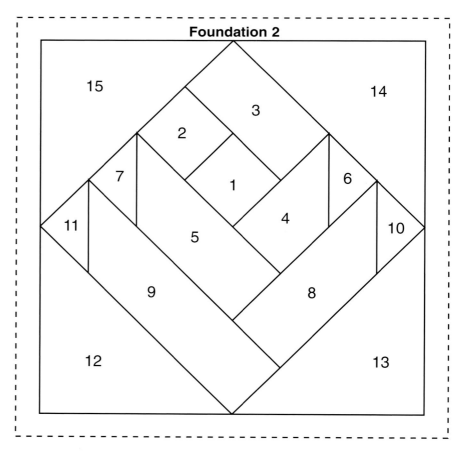

Full-Size Foundation Patterns for Flowers and Bees

(continued on page 19)

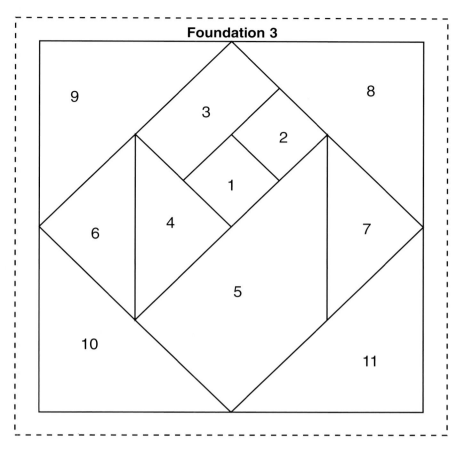

Foundation 3

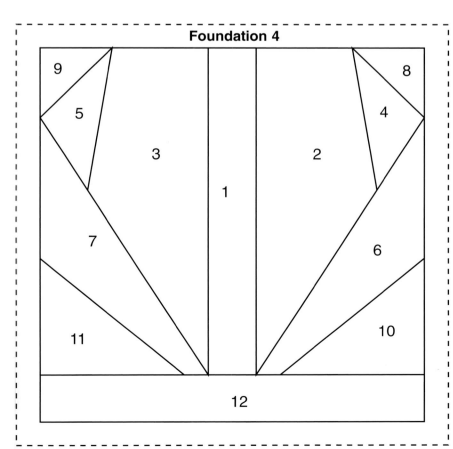

Foundation 4

Full-Size Foundation Patterns for Angels at my Window

(continued from page 13)

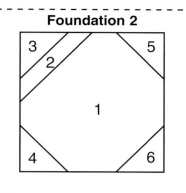

Foundation 2

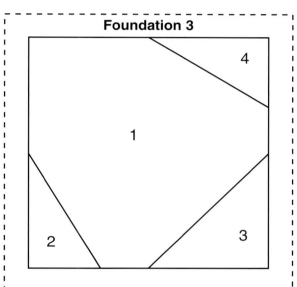

Foundation 3

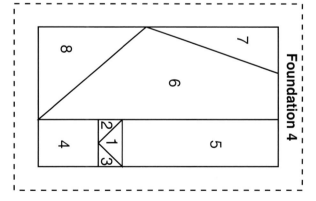

Foundation 4

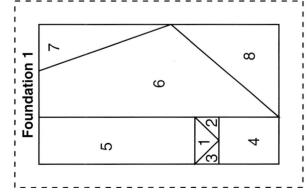

Foundation 1

Airplane Sampler

A quilt for children of all ages!

Made for a husband who hopes to get his pilot's license someday, **"Airplane Sampler"** (18" x 23") is a lively quilt that's sure to please! Stitch it in primary colors for a child's room or use blue and gray for your favorite pilot. Since each plane is pieced on a single foundation, this quilt is a snap to assemble!
(Sewn by Claudia Greiner)

QUILT SIZE: 18" x 23"
BLOCK SIZE: 4" square

MATERIALS
Yardage is estimated for 44" fabric.
• 6 prints each at least 8" x 10" for the Airplanes NOTE: *The quiltmaker used red, black, green, gold, purple and rust*
• 1/2 yard blue for the sky
• Fat eighth (11" x 18") red print
• Gold print scrap at least 3" x 4 1/2"
• 2/3 yard gradated blue print for the border
• 1/8 yard red print for the binding
• 20" x 25" piece of backing fabric
• 20" x 25" piece of thin batting
• Paper, muslin or lightweight, non-fusible interfacing for the foundations

CUTTING
Dimensions include a 1/4" seam allowance. Fabric for foundation piecing will be cut as you sew the blocks.
• Cut 17: 1 1/2" x 4 1/2" strips, red print, for the sashing
• Cut 6: 1 1/2" squares, gold print
• Cut 2: 2 1/4" x 26" strips, gradated blue print, for the border
NOTE: *To achieve the look of this quilt, cut each of the 2 1/4" x 26" strips with one end light and the other dark.*
• Cut 2: 2 1/4" x 21" strips, gradated blue print, for the border
NOTE: *Cut one of the 2 1/4" x 21" strips from the light section of the shaded print and the other from the dark section.*
• Cut 2: 1 3/4" x 44" red print strips, for the binding

DIRECTIONS
Follow the Step-by-Step Instructions *in the* General Directions *to piece the* blocks.
• Transfer the full-size pattern 12 times to the foundation material. Include all lines and numbers and leave a 1" space between foundations. Cut each one out 1/2" beyond the broken line.
For each Airplane block:
• Use the following fabrics in these positions:
  1 - print
  2, 3 - sky fabric
  4, 5 - print
  6, 7, 8 - sky fabric
  9 - print
  10, 11, 12 - sky fabric
• Baste each foundation in the seam allowance, halfway between the stitching line and the broken line.
• Trim each foundation on the broken line.
• Join three 1 1/2" x 4 1/2" red print

strips and two 1 1/2" gold print squares to make a pieced sashing strip, as shown. Make 3.

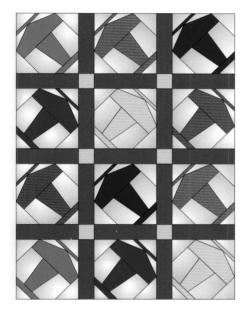

• Lay out the Airplane blocks, the pieced sashing strips and the remaining 1 1/2" x 4 1/2" red print strips. Stitch the blocks and red print strips into rows. Join the rows and pieced sashing strips, as shown in the Assembly Diagram.

• Referring to the photo for color placement, center and stitch a 2 1/4" x 26" gradated blue print strip to the long sides of the quilt. Start and stop stitching 1/4" from each edge and backstitch.
• Center and stitch a 2 1/4" x 21" gradated blue print strip to the short sides of the quilt in the same manner.
• If you used paper foundations, remove them now.
• Miter each corner, referring to the *General Directions*.
• Finish according to the *General Directions*, using the 1 3/4" red print strips for the binding.

Full-Size Foundation Pattern for Airplane Sampler

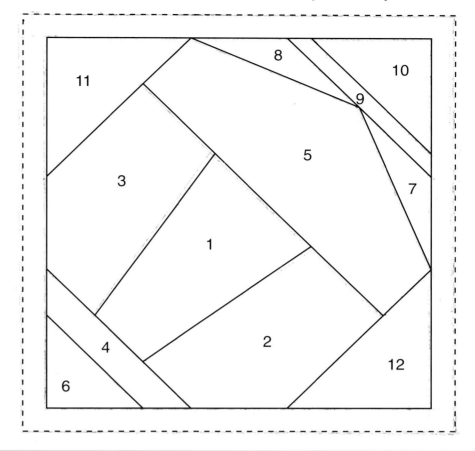

Full-Size Foundation Pattern for Flowers and Bees
(continued from page 17)

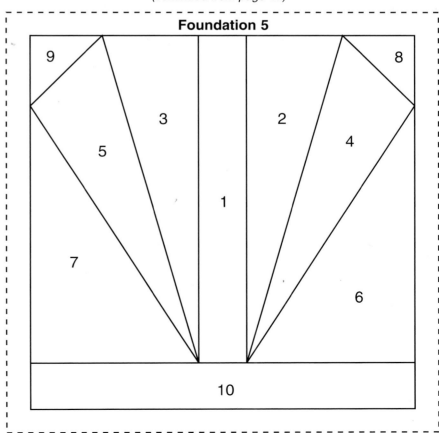

Coffee Break

*A warm addition
to your kitchen!*

Here's a great opportunity to showcase a variety of your favorite fabrics. Hang "**Coffee Break**" (18 1/2" square) in the kitchen where you can enjoy it every time you relax with your coffee or tea.
(Sewn by Alice Wilhoit)

QUILT SIZE: 18 1/2" square
COFFEE CUP BLOCK SIZE: 2" square
**COFFEE POT, PITCHER, SUGAR BOWL AND CREAMER
BLOCK SIZE:** 4" square

MATERIALS
Yardage is estimated for 44" fabric.
•   Scrap of green print at least 5" x 7"
•   Scrap of gray print at least 4 1/2" square
•   Scrap of blue print at least 5" x 6"
•   Fat quarter (18" x 22") red print for the Pitcher block and binding
•   Assorted scraps of medium and dark prints each at least 2" x 4 1/4" for the cups
•   1/2 yard white-on-white print
•   Scrap of brown at least 4 1/2" square
•   Piece of gold at least 10" square
•   Fat eighth (11" x 18") green plaid
•   20 1/2" square of backing fabric
•   20 1/2" square of thin batting
•   Paper, muslin or lightweight, non-fusible interfacing for the foundations

CUTTING
Dimensions include a 1/4" seam allowance. Fabric for foundation piecing will be cut as you sew the blocks.
•   Cut 1: 1" x 4 1/2" strip, white-on-white print
•   Cut 1: 1" x 4 1/2" strip, brown
•   Cut 2: 1 1/4" x 4 1/2" strips, brown
•   Cut 2: 1 1/2" x 8 1/2" strips, gold
•   Cut 2: 1 1/2" x 10 1/2" strips, gold
•   Cut 4: 2 1/2" squares, gold
•   Cut 4: 2 1/2" x 14 1/2" strips, green plaid, for the border
•   Cut 2: 1 3/4" x 44" strips, red print, for the binding

DIRECTIONS
Follow the Step-by-Step Instructions *in the* General Directions *to piece the blocks.*
•   Transfer the full-size patterns on pages 22 and 24 to the foundation material. Include all lines and numbers and leave a 1" space between foundations. Make one each of foundations 1 through 10.

Make 24 of foundation 11. Cut each one out 1/2" beyond the broken line.
•   Use the following fabrics in these positions:
For foundation 1:
    1 - white-on-white print
    2, 3, 4 - green print
    5, 6, 7 - white-on-white print
    8 - green print
For foundation 2:
    1 - green print
    2 - white-on-white print
For foundation 3:
    1 - green print
    2, 3 - white-on-white print
    4 - green print
    5, 6 - white-on-white print
•   Baste each foundation in the seam allowance, halfway between the stitching line and the broken line.
•   Trim each foundation on the broken line.
•   Lay out foundations 1, 2 and 3 and the 1" x 4 1/2" brown strip. Join them to make the Coffee Pot block. Set it aside.

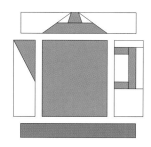

For foundation 4:
   1 - gray print
   2, 3, 4, 5, 6, - white-on-white print

For foundation 5:
   1 - gray print
   2, 3 - white-on-white print
   4 - brown
• Baste and trim each foundation, as before.
• Lay out foundations 4 and 5. Join them to make the Sugar Bowl block. Set it aside.

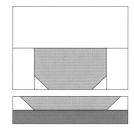

For foundation 6:
   1 - white-on-white print
   2, 3, 4 - blue print
   5, 6 - white-on-white print
   7 - blue print

For foundation 7:
   1 - white-on-white print
   2, 3, 4 - blue print
   5, 6 - white-on-white print

For foundation 8:
   1 - blue print
   2, 3 - white-on-white print
   4 - blue print
   5, 6, 7 - white-on-white print
• Baste and trim each foundation.
• Lay out foundations 6, 7 and 8 and a 1 1/4" x 4 1/2" brown strip. Join them to make the Creamer block. If necessary, trim the block to measure 4 1/2" from top to bottom. Set it aside.

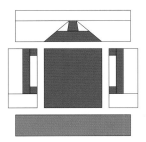

For foundation 9:
   1 - white-on-white print
   2, 3, 4 - red print
   5, 6, 7 - white-on-white print
   8 - red print

For foundation 10:
   1 - white-on-white print
   2 - red print
• Baste and trim each foundation.
• Lay out foundations 9 and 10. Join them. Stitch the 1" x 4 1/2" white-on-white print strip to the top of the unit and the remaining 1 1/4" x 4 1/2" brown strip to the bottom to make the Pitcher block. Set it aside.

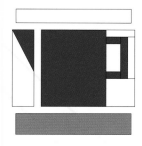

For foundation 11:
   1 - white-on-white print
   2, 3, 4 - print
   5, 6 - white-on-white print
   7 - same print
   8, 9, 10 - white-on-white print
• Baste and trim each foundation.

ASSEMBLY
• Referring to the photo, lay out the Coffee Pot, Sugar Bowl, Creamer and Pitcher blocks. Join them to make the quilt center.
• Stitch the 1 1/2" x 8 1/2" gold strips to the sides of the quilt center.
• Stitch the 1 1/2" x 10 1/2" gold strips to the top and bottom of the quilt center.
• Referring to the Assembly Diagram, lay out the quilt center and the Coffee Cups. Arrange the Coffee Cups in any color order you like, then stitch them into vertical and horizontal rows, as shown.
• Stitch the vertical rows to the sides of the quilt.
• Stitch the horizontal rows to the top and bottom of the quilt.
• Stitch two 2 1/2" x 14 1/2" green plaid strips to the sides of the quilt.
• Stitch a 2 1/2" gold square to each end of a 2 1/2" x 14 1/2" green plaid strip. Make 2.
• Stitch these pieced strips to the top and bottom of the quilt.
• If you used paper foundations, remove them now.
• Finish according to the *General Directions*, using the 1 3/4" red print strips for the binding.

Full-Size Patterns for Coffee Break begin on page 22

Assembly Diagram

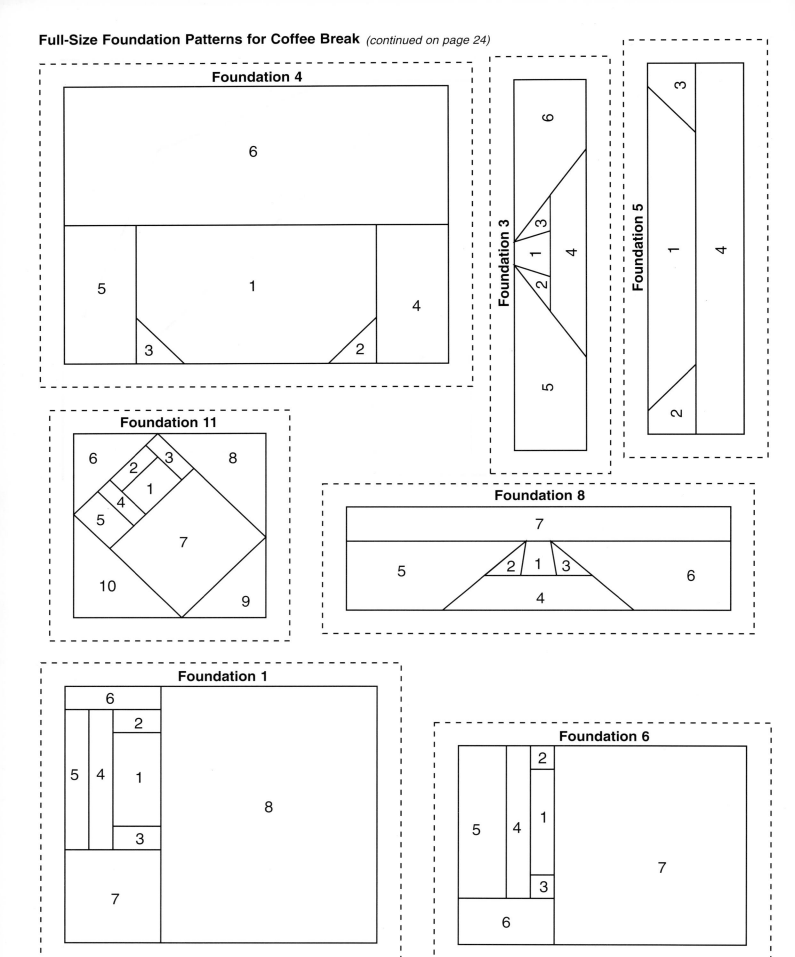

Sailboats

Stormy skies and full sails make an intriguing mini!

I achieved the "calm before the storm" look in this quilt with the use of hand dyed Bali fabrics. **"Sailboats"** (22" square) is sure to be a favorite nautical mini!

QUILT SIZE: 22" square
BLOCK SIZE: 4" square

MATERIALS
Yardage is estimated for 44" fabric.
• Assorted print scraps for the boats and sails
• 1/4 yard sky fabric
• 1/8 yard medium blue, for the sea
• 1/2 yard black, for the sashing and outer border
• 1/4 yard dark blue, for the binding
• 24" square of backing fabric
• 24" square of thin batting
• Paper, muslin or lightweight, non-fusible interfacing for the foundations

CUTTING
Dimensions include a 1/4" seam allowance. Fabric for foundation piecing will be cut as you sew the blocks.
• Cut 6: 1 1/2" x 4 1/2" strips, black, for the sashing
• Cut 4: 1 1/2" x 14 1/2" strips, black, for the sashing
• Cut 2: 1 1/2" x 16 1/2" strips, black,

for the sashing
• Cut 2: 2 3/4" x 19 1/2" strips, black, for the outer border
• Cut 2: 2 3/4" x 24" strips, black, for the outer border
• Cut 2: 1" x 18 1/2" strips, sky fabric, for the inner border
• Cut 2: 1" x 19 1/2" strips, sky fabric, for the inner border
• Cut 3: 1 3/4" x 44" strips, dark blue, for the binding

DIRECTIONS
Follow the Step-by-Step Instructions *in the* General Directions *to piece the blocks.*
• Transfer the full-size pattern 9 times to the foundation material. Include all lines and numbers and leave a 1" space between foundations. Cut each one out 1/2" beyond the broken line.
For each Sailboat block:
• Use the following fabrics in these positions:
    1 - sail scrap
    2, 3 - sky fabric

4 - same sail scrap
5, 6, 7, 8 - sky fabric
9 - boat scrap
10, 11 - sky fabric
12 - medium blue
• Baste each foundation in the seam allowance, halfway between the stitching line and the broken line.
• Trim each foundation on the broken line.
• Lay out the sailboat blocks and the 1 1/2" x 4 1/2" black sashing strips, as shown.

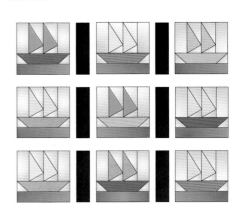

(continued on page 24)

23

- Join the blocks and strips to make horizontal rows.
- Lay out the rows and 1 1/2" x 14 1/2" black sashing strips and join them, as shown.

- Stitch the 1 1/2" x 16 1/2" black sashing strips to the sides of the quilt.
- Measure the length of the quilt. Trim the 1" x 18 1/2" tan strips to equal that measurement.
- Stitch them to the sides of the quilt.
- Measure the width of the quilt including the borders. Trim the 1" x 19 1/2" sky fabric strips to equal that measurement.
- Stitch them to the top and bottom of the quilt.
- In the same manner, trim the 2 3/4" x 19 1/2" black strips to fit the quilt's

length and stitch them to the sides of the quilt.
- Trim the 2 3/4" x 24" black strips to fit the quilt's width and stitch them to the top and bottom of the quilt.

- If you used paper foundations, remove them now.
- Finish according to the *General Directions*, using the 1 3/4" dark blue strips for the binding.

Full-Size Foundation Pattern for Sailboats

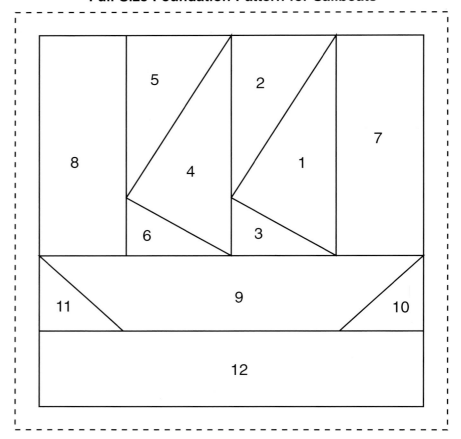

Full-Size Foundation Patterns for Coffee Break

(continued from page 22)

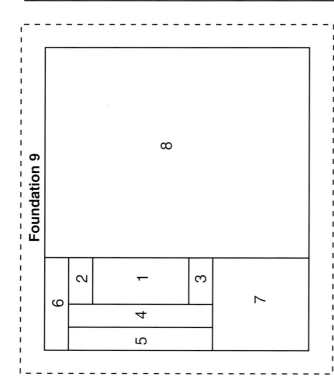

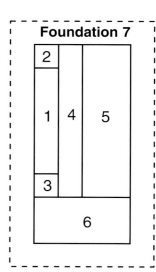

Outstanding in the Field

Shhh! You can almost hear them moo!

"Outstanding in the Field" (18 1/2" square) is a whimsical quilt for everyone who appreciates the charms of the bovine family. Stitch these little cows in your favorite prints and enjoy their company anytime.
(Sewn by Sue Miklos-Champion)

QUILT SIZE: 18 1/2" square
BLOCK SIZE: 4" square

MATERIALS
Yardage is estimated for 44" fabric.
• 9 brown, rust and burgundy print scraps each at least 3 1/2" x 6", for the cows
• 9 pink scraps each at least 1 1/2" square
• 1/4 yard light print for the background
• 1/3 yard brown print for the sashing and binding
• 1/8 yard brown plaid
• Second brown print scrap at least 3" square
• 20 1/2" square of backing fabric
• 20 1/2" square of thin batting
• Paper, muslin or lightweight, non-fusible interfacing for the foundations

CUTTING
Dimensions include a 1/4" seam allowance. Fabric for foundation piecing will be cut as you sew the blocks.
• Cut 2: 1 3/4" x 44" strips, brown print, for the binding
• Cut 12: 1 1/2" x 4 1/2" strips, brown print, for the sashing
• Cut 4: 1 1/2" x 14 1/2" strips, brown print, for the inner border
• Cut 8: 1 1/2" squares, brown plaid
• Cut 4: 1 1/2" x 16 1/2" strips, brown plaid, for the outer border
• Cut 4: 1 1/2" squares, second brown print

DIRECTIONS
Follow the Step-by-Step Instructions *in the* General Directions *to piece the blocks.*
• Transfer the full-size patterns to the foundation material. Include all lines and numbers and leave a 1" space between foundations. Make 9 each of foundations 4, 5 and 6 on page 26. Cut each one out 1/2" beyond the broken line.

For each Cow block:
• Use the following fabrics in these positions:
For foundation 4:
   1 - cow print
   2, 3 - light print
   4 - same cow print
   5, 6 - light print
For foundation 5:
   1 - light print
   2 - pink print
   3 - light print
   4, 5, 6 - same cow print
   7 - light print
For foundation 6:
   1 - light print
   2 - same cow print
   3 - light print
• Baste each foundation in the seam allowance, halfway between the stitching line and the broken line.
• Trim each foundation on the broken line.
• Lay out foundations 4, 5 and 6. Join

(continued on page 26)

them to make a Cow block. Make 9.

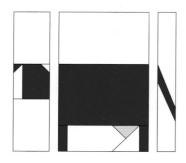

ASSEMBLY

• Lay out 3 Cow blocks and two 1 1/2" x 4 1/2" brown print strips. Join them to make a row. Make 3.

• Lay out three 1 1/2" x 4 1/2" brown print strips and two 1 1/2" brown plaid squares. Join them to make a sashing strip. Make 2.

• Referring to the photo, lay out the rows and sashing strips. Join them.
• Stitch two 1 1/2" x 14 1/2" brown print strips to the sides of the quilt.
• Stitch a 1 1/2" brown plaid square to each end of a 1 1/2" x 14 1/2" gold print strip. Make 2.
• Stitch these pieced strips to the top and bottom of the quilt.
• Stitch two 1 1/2" x 16 1/2" brown plaid strips to the sides of the quilt.
• Stitch a 1 1/2" brown print square to each end of a 1 1/2" x 16 1/2" brown plaid strip. Make 2.
• Stitch these pieced strips to the top and bottom of the quilt.
• If you used paper foundations, remove them now.
• Finish according to the *General Directions*, using the 1 3/4" brown print strips for the binding.

Full-Size Foundation Patterns for Outstanding in the Field and Home for Milking

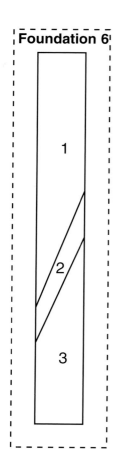

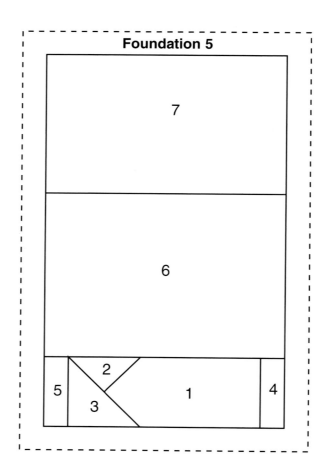

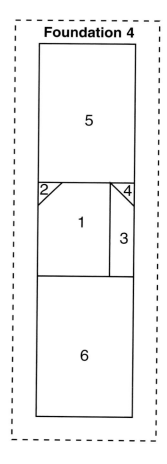

Home for Milking

A quilt for anyone who loves the country!

Bring the great outdoors inside with **"Home for Milking"** (26 1/2" x 16 1/2"). A quilt this cute is at home in the country or city and will surely get attention. (Sewn by Rosalyn Constant)

QUILT SIZE: 16 1/2" x 26 1/2"
BARN BLOCK SIZE: 7 1/2" square
COW BLOCK SIZE: 4" square
TREE BLOCK SIZE: 2" square

MATERIALS
Yardage is estimated for 44" fabric.
- 1/2 yard beige print
- First burgundy print at least 10" square for the barn
- Brown print scrap at least 3 1/2" square
- Yellow scrap at least 5" x 6"
- Gold stripe scrap at least 3 1/2" x 10"
- Second burgundy print at least 6" x 9" for the cows
- Pink print scrap at least 1 1/2" x 3"
- Dark brown scrap at least 3" x 4 1/2" for the tree trunks
- First green print scrap at least 9" x 10" for the trees
- Second green print scrap at least 3 1/2" x 12"
- Third green print scrap at least 5 1/2" x 7 1/2"
- Tan print strip at least 1" x 20"
- 1/3 yard blue print
- 1/4 yard burgundy for the binding
- 18 1/2" x 28 1/2" piece of backing fabric
- 18 1/2" x 28 1/2" piece of thin batting

- Paper, muslin or lightweight, non-fusible interfacing for the foundations

CUTTING
Dimensions include a 1/4" seam allowance. Fabric for foundation piecing will be cut as you sew the blocks.
- Cut 2: 1 3/4" x 8 1/2" strips, beige print
- Cut 1: 1" x 12 1/2" strip, beige print
- Cut 2: 2 1/2" x 22 1/2" strips, beige print
- Cut 1: 1" x 20" strip, tan print
- Cut 3: 1 3/4" x 36" strips, burgundy, for the binding
- Cut 2: 1 1/2" x 26 1/2" strips, blue print
- Cut 2: 1 1/2" x 14 1/2" strips, blue print
- Cut 4: 1 1/2" squares, blue print

DIRECTIONS
Follow the Step-by-Step Instructions *in the* General Directions *to piece the blocks.*
- Transfer the full-size patterns to the foundation material. Include all lines and numbers and leave a 1" space between foundations. Make one each of foundations 1 and 3. Make 2 of foundation 2. Make 3 each of foundations 4, 5 and 6

(page 26). Make 6 each of foundations 7 and 8. Make 34 of foundation 9. Cut each one out 1/2" beyond the broken line.
- Use the following fabrics in these positions:
For foundation 1:
    1 - first burgundy print
    2, 3, 4, 5 - beige print
For the first foundation 2:
    1 - same burgundy print
    2, 3 - gold stripe
    4, 5 - same burgundy print
For the second foundation 2:
    1 - yellow
    2, 3 - gold stripe
    4, 5 - same burgundy print
For foundation 3:
    1 - yellow
    2, 3 - gold stripe
    4, 5 - brown print
    6, 7 - same burgundy print
- Baste each foundation in the seam allowance, halfway between the stitching line and the broken line.
- Trim each foundation on the broken line.
- Lay out foundation 1, both foundation 2's and a foundation 3, as shown. Join them to make the Barn block. Set it aside.

(continued on page 28)

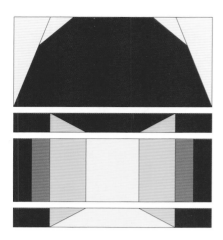

For foundation 4:
   1 - second burgundy print
   2, 3 - beige print
   4 - same burgundy print
   5, 6 - beige print

For foundation 5:
   1 - beige print
   2 - pink print
   3 - beige print
   4, 5, 6 - same burgundy print
   7 - beige print

For foundation 6:
   1 - beige print
   2 - same burgundy print
   3 - beige print

• Baste and trim each foundation as before.
• Lay out one each of foundations 4, 5 and 6. Join them to make a Cow block. Make 3.

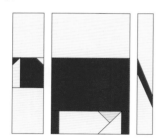

• Referring to the photo, join the Cow blocks to form a Cow row. Set it aside.

For foundation 7:
   1 - dark brown
   2, 3 - beige print
   4 - first green print
   5, 6 - beige print
   7 - same green print
   8, 9 - beige print
   10 - same green print
   11, 12 - beige print
   13 - same green print
   14, 15, 16, 17 - beige print

For foundation 8:
   1 - second green print

   2 - beige print
   3 - third green print
   4 - beige print
   5 - second green print

• Baste and trim each foundation.
• Lay out a foundation 7 and a foundation 8, as shown. Join them to make a tree unit. Make 6.

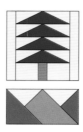

• Join them to make a Tree row. Set it aside.

For foundation 9:
   1 - beige print
   2, 3 - blue print

• Baste and trim each foundation. Set them aside.
• Stitch the 1" x 12 1/2" beige print strip to the top of the Tree row.
• Referring to the photo, lay out the Barn block, the Cow row and the Tree row. Join the rows.
• Stitch the 1" x 20" tan print strip to the bottom of the unit to form the quilt center.
• Stitch a 1 3/4" x 8 1/2" beige print strip to each side of the quilt.
• Stitch a 2 1/2" x 22 1/2" beige print strip to the top and bottom of the quilt.
• Lay out 6 foundation 9's. Join them to form a short border. Make 2. Stitch

Full-Size Foundation Patterns for Home for Milking

a 1 1/2" blue print square to each end of these short borders. Set them aside.

• Lay out 11 foundation 9's. Join them to form a long border. Make 2.
• Stitch the long borders to the top and bottom of the quilt, keeping the base of the beige triangle against the quilt.
• Stitch the short borders to the sides of the quilt.
• Stitch the 1 1/2" x 14 1/2" blue print strips to the sides of the quilt.
• Stitch the 1 1/2" x 26 1/2" blue print strips to the top and bottom of the quilt.
• If you used paper foundations, remove them now.
• Finish according to the *General Directions*, using the 1 3/4" burgundy strips for the binding.

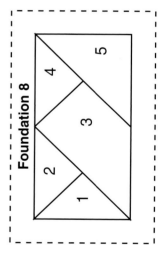

Foundation 8

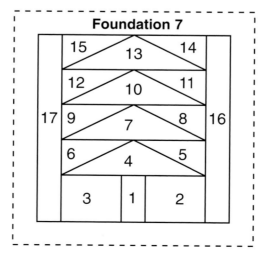

Foundation 7

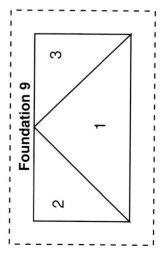

Foundation 9

Foundation 1

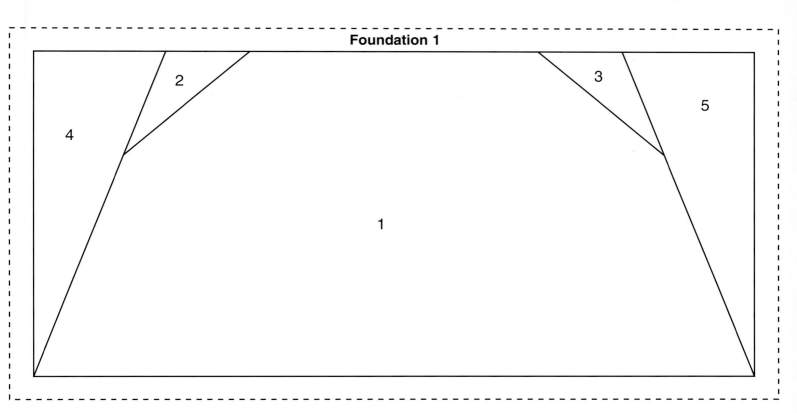

Foundation 2

Foundation 3

Bless This House

Add a little coziness and warmth to your home!

"Bless This House" (12 1/2" x 24 1/2") imbues a peaceful feeling in any home. The colors give the viewer a sense of warmth and the lights in the windows say "somebody's home!" This little quilt would be a perfect housewarming or wedding shower gift.

QUILT SIZE: 12 1/2" x 24 1/2"
HOUSE BLOCK SIZE: 4" square
TREE BLOCK SIZE: 3" x 4"
LETTER BLOCK SIZE: 1" square

MATERIALS
Yardage is estimated for 44" fabric.
• 3 burgundy print scraps for the houses
• 2 black print scraps for the tree trunks
• 6 red, burgundy and rust print scraps for the roofs
• 6 gold and brown print scraps for the windows and doors
• Assorted green print scraps totaling 1/4 yard for the Flying Geese and trees
• 1/8 yard solid burgundy for the letters
• 1/2 yard light print for the background
• 1/4 yard gold plaid for the borders
• 1/8 yard red print for the binding
• 14 1/2" x 26 1/2" piece of backing fabric
• 14 1/2" x 26 1/2" piece of thin batting
• Paper, muslin or lightweight, non-fusible interfacing for the foundations

CUTTING
Dimensions include a 1/4" seam allowance. Fabric for foundation piecing will be cut as you sew the blocks.
• Cut 1: 1 1/2" x 18 1/2" strip, light print
• Cut 8: A, light print
• Cut 8: 1 1/2" squares, light print
• Cut 2: 1 1/2" x 24 1/2" strips, gold plaid, for the outer border
• Cut 2: 1 1/2" x 18 1/2" strips, gold plaid, for the inner border
• Cut 2: 1 1/2" x 10 1/2" strips, gold plaid, for the outer border
• Cut 2: 1 1/2" x 8 1/2" strips, gold plaid, for the inner border
• Cut 2: 1 3/4" x 44" strips, red print, for the binding

DIRECTIONS
Follow the Step-by-Step Instructions *in the* General Directions *to piece the blocks.*
• Transfer the full-size patterns to the foundation material. Include all lines and numbers and leave a 1" space between foundations. Make one each of foundations 4, 5, 6, 10, 12, 13 and 14. Make 2 each of foundations 3, 7 and 11. Make 3 each of foundations 1 and 2. Make 4 each of foundations 8 and 9. Make 14 of foundation 15. Cut each one out 1/2" beyond the broken line.
• Use the following fabrics in these positions:
For foundation 1:
  1 - red, burgundy or rust print
  2 - different red, burgundy or rust print
  3, 4, 5 - light print
For foundation 2:
  1 - gold plaid

  2, 3, 4, 5 - one burgundy print
  6 - different gold or brown print
  7, 8 - same burgundy print
For foundation 3:
  1 - black print
  2, 3 - light print
  4 - green print
  5, 6 - light print
  7 - green print
  8, 9 - light print
  10 - green print
  11, 12 - light print
  13 - green print
  14, 15, 16, 17, 18 - light print
For foundations 4 through 14:
• Piece each foundation in numerical order, using solid red for the shaded sections and light print for the remaining sections.
For foundation 15:
• Piece each foundation in numerical order, using assorted green prints for the shaded sections and the light background print for the remaining sections.
• Baste each foundation in the seam allowance, halfway between the stitching line and the broken line.
• Trim each foundation on the broken line.

ASSEMBLY
• Lay out a foundation 1 and a foundation 2. Join them to make a House block. Make 3.